The Other Revival

"Salaam Green teaches history, with all of its vexing and painful details, in elegant poetic form. The stories and images she shares in verse testify to the remarkable resilience of Black Americans (Alabamians to be precise.) Honest, vulnerable, insightful, and hopeful, Green's poems are soul food."

— **IMANI PERRY**, author of *Black in Blues: How a Color Tells the Story of My People*

"I want every county in the United States to somehow engage in this kind of collaborative poetic anthropology—one that crosses boundaries of race, age, and gender."

— **ANDY FOGLE**, author of *Mother Countries* and poetry editor at *Salvation South*

"Through reclamation, inquisition, & quilting, Green's collection keeps history soaring, flying, & affecting us right here in the present. *The Other Revival* adds another dimension to Alabama's canon of documentary poetics."

— **NABILA LOVELACE**, author of *Sons of Achilles*

"This collection is history, remnant, and connection chronicled in poetry that is as nuanced and tender as it is necessary for reconciliation and healing."

—**JACQUELINE TRIMBLE**, author of *American Happiness and How to Survive the Apocalypse*

©2025 Salaam Green

ISBN 979-8-9902208-7-4

Published by Pulley Press,
an imprint of
Clyde Hill Publishing

Cover and book design by Dan D Shafer

The Other Revival

Poems & Reckonings

SALAAM GREEN

PULLEY
PRESS

For Mr. Albert "Peter" Datcher

Contents

THE WOMAN IN THE YELLOW APRON

THE WOMAN IN THE YELLOW APRON
DEPARTS FOR A TENT REVIVAL

ROAD TO THE HISTORY HOUSE

THE WALLACE HOUSE

A Preface

MY NAME IS SALAAM GREEN. I am a poet and native of Greensboro, Alabama, and a longtime resident of Birmingham, Alabama. In 2024, I became the first poet laureate of the city. My home places are in the "Civil Rights Belt," a swath of land that runs from Alabama to Kansas. For four years, I have been working in the community of Harpersville, Alabama—a town haunted by the former Wallace House plantation.

Samuel Wallace built the Wallace House in 1841 with thirty-nine people whom he brought in captivity from Virginia. These enslaved people were kept by Wallace and his wife, forced to construct the house and work the land. Originally, Samuel Wallace had come to Alabama as a soldier serving under Andrew Jackson and had probably fought in the Battle of Horseshoe Bend in 1814. That battle forced the Creek Nation to cede 23 million acres, half of central Alabama, and a large swath of southern Georgia, to the United States government. Wallace had history in Alabama, and he built on it with the labor of people who were enslaved by him.

For generations, the house remained in the Wallace family. Samuel Henderson Wallace, a descendant and physician from Birmingham, planned to retire to the house but died before he could. His widow, Nell J. Wallace, lived in the house during the 1950s. After that, the house was mostly vacant except for occasional weekend use by the family.

In 2018, Nell Gottlieb, the fourth great-granddaughter of Samuel Wallace, inherited the house. She and Theoangelo Perkins, the mayor of Harpersville, became cofounders of an organization to promote healing from the history of enslavement in that place. Perkins' Black Mcginnis ancestors came to the Wallace farm after emancipation and have been connected with the Wallaces over generations. Together, Nell and Theoangelo created the Klein Arts & Culture Center and, in 2019, deeded the house and associated six acres to that nonprofit organization. In 2023, the organization was renamed the Wallace Center for Arts and Reconciliation, and became a nonprofit that promotes reconciliation, healing, and repair through arts, education, and cultural programming.

That year, I helped convene the annual "Homecoming" to the Wallace House. I met people on both the enslavers' and enslaved peoples' descendent lines. What was startling and eventually consoling was how many of these folks craved healing. They wanted to tell their own stories of experiencing racially motivated abuse and structural racism; others wanted to reflect on how they had participated as active or passive abusers of others. Since that first gathering, the Homecomings are annual events in which any descendents can come together and find ways to heal and reflect.

As I became more and more involved with the house, my own work as a poet and healer grew more urgent. In 2020, I became a Certified Listener Poet through the Good Listening Project. This helped me to listen deeply and support people who are telling their stories. I worked as a teaching writer with the Alabama Writers Forum, and I created and edited an anthology of poetry for sixth grade students to write poems in response to both Black and white descendants of the Wallace House. When the children completed their poems and we published them in the *Voyages From the Writing Our Stories Project*, I invited them to come and read their work at the Wallace House. Teachers, family members, and friends from the community of Vincent Middle and High School in Vincent, Alabama arrived at the former plantation. This was the first time the sixth grade students had entered the house or the grounds of the Wallace House. I remember how curious they were. They wanted to go upstairs, see the attic and explore the grounds. The expansive front porch was the backdrop for a class photo at the end of the day. I still look at that photograph and think of those young poets.

For me, that started something. I was drawn to the Wallace House as a place, and as a place where you could encounter a painful history and reflect upon it. I went on to host workshops and gatherings for descendants of the enslaved and enslavers, as well as local historians, neighbors, and community folk. I served in a poet residency at the former plantation.

Over two years, in 2023 – 2024, I interviewed sixteen Black and white descendants, including current board members, people who still live in Harpersville, and the white descendants of the enslavers who inherited the house and land. In some cases, both have the last name "Wallace."

Those interviews, along with my own journey coming to terms with my work at the former plantation and my discovery of Peter Datcher's own "History House" grew into the book of poems you now hold in your hands.

Our conversations took place in Harpersville and Creswell, Alabama. They happened at the Wallace House, History House, the local community center, and in many Black descendants' homes and on front porches in the community. Many of the interviews of the enslaved descendants took place during the first Juneteenth celebration in 2023. This was the first time that these Black descendants convened on the land without white descendants. Other interviews took place during Homecoming 2023 when descendants came from as far away as California, Oklahoma, Illinois, Texas, Wisconsin, and Washington DC.

Peter Datcher, one of the oldest Black descendants and the family keeper of stories, points to the urgency of these convenings: "We as people of color, need to look at our ancestry and white people, too, to find out what our people did and who we are and what they accomplished... My grandmother was born in 1870. Her name was Rachel Baker Datcher. She passed on a lot of history to my mother and aunt. That's how I heard a lot of things. I didn't realize what I was hearing until I started doing the history and started reading some things. God, I've already known this."

I was haunted and moved by the idea that so much is passed on to the living. I also found joy in the many stories of resistance. *The Other Revival* brings together quotes from my interviews with the Wallace Plantation descendents, observations of that place, and my own sensibilities as a poet. After I created drafts, I worked with the descendants to assure that the poems are as they would like them. I think of it as a rare and unique approach in gathering the voices of people whose ancestors lived at the Wallace House Plantation, that farming town at the foot of the early east – west railroad that connected the deep south with the west. It's a place where life goes on, reaching out and beyond the past.

HISTORY HOUSE

"It's about my ancestors. I've done a few things.
My ancestors have done much more."

–Peter Datcher, living Black Descendant of Wallace House
Plantation, from transcripts on Juneteenth 2023

One of the things that Peter Datcher has done was
to create his own History House. This place is the
first house in Shelby County to be owned by a Black
family. Peter has collected his own artifacts and
tours visitors through.

Back *to the* Plantation

All over Again, I Go

I work at a plantation house
I go there to perform

the 2024 version

of *plantation house* and I
wonder about my performance

of 1854

and the others who also
performed for real

all those years in between

the women who were poets
who never had an opportunity

to write a poem but knew
that they were poets

in that plantation house
where they weren't heard

I am a *descendent*
a word that wraps me into them

Taking White People on Tours of Cotton Fields

(WITH NELL GOTTLIEB)

I start to feel like a tour guide
to a place where my ancestors were held captive.
Folks from the north who haven't ever seen
cotton fields might expect southerners
to tour with them through the sticky weeds.
We people in the deep south pass
by plantation land all our lives.
Cotton survives in the heat,
flowering buds in the Fall.

Those who are curious cajole us
back to the field's edge, along that river
where shadows survive the past,
time is a petal dangling to be free,
cotton blooming into speech,
fields resisting freedom's call.

Sam Wallace and His Wife

Once upon a time and way back when
Sam Wallace of Virginia
brought enslaved persons
to Harpersville
miles and miles on the wagon trail
migrating from one big house to a new big house.

*What an amazing soliloquy, a cute and quaint children's song
so false, so misleading. I perform instead this version:*

Except humanity, Sam Wallace and his wife
brought everything with them from Virginia.
Except humanity, they transported people,
living beings with souls.
Mr. and Mrs. Sam Wallace
brought that wretched world
which slavery protected—
the stench of labor to break
the backs of the tender.
They brought them unfree to Alabama
a place rich in many things.
Except humanity.

We Some Kin

(WITH NELL GOTTLEIB)

You and I are family
I want to be weightless
as fuel for a soul's fire
I want to know what comfort can do
Meet me underneath the tree

A Poem for Descendant Babies Who Hide in Trees: Viola's Burial Party

Death called everyone home to visit
underneath the tree where enslaved relatives
were "broke in" to punish the living.
Little Viola didn't live long
her umbilical cord choked hope
and her mother willed herself to stay alive
when she placed the baby in a small pine box.

Others came to console her:
They were mothers too—
some with wombs, and some without.
They stitched a tiny multicolored dress that slipped
over the ghost baby's body
like animal fiber from a silkworm tree
Mama Birds danced as the moon sang to the mystic sky.
After burying of the baby
women served warm tea and
leafy cooked greens and greasy fatback.
The eating felt like a rebirth.

Outside Harpersville, a Ghost Bicycle

(WITH ANGIE ODEN)

On the road to the Wallace House
next to a field is
an old white bicycle
decorated with plastic
flowers, faded now.
A ghost bicycle left
after someone died
riding here.
The bicycle leans against
a tree to decorate this ground
as if the ancestors glided
the bicycle down
from heaven and placed it
on this road in Shelby County
where all of us passersby would
know that bicycles have wings.
My own red glider—
polka dots and butterfly flaps,
mud guards made of silk—
that bicycle would pedal me
to a heaven where one tire swing
hangs from a saving grace
tree. Underneath, a place
to park any bicycle and give
it wings, just after it descended
from that same glorious sky.

Back to the Plantation

The road to the Wallace Plantation is familiar,
as all back roads are to me.
My body is levitating   Outside of itself.

I am the cotton, grown and ready for picking.
To roll the windows down and be fascinated by cotton,
I am expected to see that cotton could be beautiful
and is beautiful—the way that the sunrays shine
is beautiful the way that the shadows end the day

is mesmerizing. I'm expected to know
those things and recognize those things.
Cotton is not something I want to see,
when I'm expected to perform at a plantation house.

Cotton in Harpersville on a Beautiful Day, Again

May this be the last word about the beauty of cotton,
May this dethrone its ugly, painful past.

How cotton causes one to hold the breath
How cotton causes many to bend and slow down

Once they come into the fields.
Once the bolls so small and the view so wide,

Cotton, Cotton—can't get the words to come out of the throat.
Cotton, every syllable that can't soften trouble.

Remnant

(WITH HYDEIA AVERETT)

Thistle of a town,
in the soaked skin of rural America—
Elemental with red clay
and barrels stacked up
lonely looking and empty.
Where's the energy of a relationship
with the past? Frantic and lost,
it gallops off,
a deer in a void
of distance, far from its place.

What I Will Tell My Sixth-Grade Students About My Family Trip

(WITH DANIEL BOATNER V.)

I went to protect the ones who lived
in the midst of it.
The ones who worked at invasive planting,
who worked at cotton.

I want to polish the reputations of the worthy
to set the furniture straight in the living room
to put the bread back into the oven
so it could brown perfectly.

I went because
I can't teach what I don't know and
I can't teach what I haven't acknowledged.
I want my sixth graders to believe
that they are part of the progressing history of America
and that they can't ever be erased.
What I want for my students
I want for myself, therefore I go South.

At the
Wallace House
Plantation

Can I Go In?

(WITH PETER DATCHER)

On Juneteenth, 2023—First Black Descendants' Day

When a Black descendant arrives at the Wallace House,
They'll step onto the splintered porch and say

Can I go in?
As if the weathered ceilings would fall down

Can I go in
that bedroom where the door is painted shut?

Can I pass through
the cigarette smoke baked into the walls?

Can I go into
the enslavement house without falling dizzy?

When a Black descendent goes in, they ask:
Which entrance would I pass through now?
The one for us, the one for them?

This Place could never be a home
but a holding cell, wired and shut down

unable to contain all the spirits
waiting to greet each of us.

Homecomings in Harpersville

(WITH DORIS MCLEOD-WILLIAMS)

In Harpersville the lilies rise
firecrackers pop in someone's backyard

Homecoming can feel like spitting out watermelon seeds
on the front porch where grandfather
coughed up blood from his lung cancer.

Selling Babies in Shelby County

(WITH PETER DATCHER)

Dirt could run up and over a mountain
before a slave mother could see her child again

In Shelby County, the sale of a baby
could buy a pretty calf or more land
for a white woman's inheritance

Selling babies in Alabama financed
more plantation property
Healthy, fat babies and first born children
handed away for dollars and dimes

Groomed for hire, for ungodly servitude—
taught to put the wash out
before they could speak
They were raggedy dolls for white children

Some carried the blue eyes of white daddies.
In the backyard quarters where the moon
hid from the earth
Can you hear the crying of those mothers?

Of the land where the crash of the ax marked
the hard dirt?

The Size of a Full Moon at the Wallace Plantation House

(WITH ANGIE ODEN & BEVERLY JOHNSON, SISTERS)

After my mother died
a cocoon kept me

hiding

I was water
and cornbread

How could I lift
myself and the kin

of this place
from roots of injustice

Black descendants
descendants white

When I returned
a black butterfly landed

A tiny full moon
of blue wings

flitting over these shoulders
Our ancestors are here

To welcome

the hunger and
lightness of our touch.

Pouring of the Water:
A Ritual at Wallace House

2023: A Young Black Boy Writes the Name of the Enslaved

Here at the edges, in a room dim
with yellow clay wallpaper,
a Black boy's joy alights.

After he writes the name of the man
once enslaved here, the boy puts
the paper into the water bucket

and releases the water back to the earth.
He's a scribe who reminds
all the Black children who walked barefoot

on Wallace Plantation and pushed
water jugs too heavy
to keep pouring until every drop reaches inside

the dead limbs of these trees.
Keep pouring Black boy joy until
the joy, Black boy, you can't pour no more.

Lovers & Lanterns:
How Our Ancestors Found Each Other
(WITH DANIEL BOATNER V.)

So kind are these small niche love stories.
The tenderness of making sure
the lantern is lit
when heat meant suffering
and desire felt cold.
Enslaved people were lovers
and as they caught light
moonlight washed those
ghost bodies with the flame
of an unrushed hope.

An Unlovely Bequeath

(WITH NELL GOTTLIEB)

I inherited the house
a litany of woes
that whisper
"A plantation by any other name"
is a Plantation—
still a litany of woes.

As a white girl playing
knowing the difference
wondering if our child feet could
escape our need for one another—
The connections are coarse and humble.

Washing the White Out:
A Lullaby for the Ones Left Behind

Enslavers played one
Whitewashing a world for fun
Enslavers played two
Putting fear in more than a few
Enslavers played three
Lynching humans on a tree

Descendants played one
Washing out the white and becoming the sun
Descendants played two
Washing the white out and naming the world anew
Descendants played three
Washing the white out to be
Radically, essentially, free.

Plantation Expanse

(WITH NELL GOTTLIEB)

What does 5,000 acres of plantation look like?
Some might say it's "a large acreage farm"
of soybeans blooming yellow
dandelion and chicory root binding
mud, grassy decay

If land can stretch wide and wondrous
brassy weeds fickle and fraying

What should the ancestors conjure on this land
   Vengeance or Victor
      Peacemaker or Sergeant

Give us each an acre instead. Give it as homage
to the sad land that conjures
fire and mud
soon to be
fertile and ripe
 but never common ground.

Redeeming a Relic—
Reclaiming a Storied Past

(WITH NELL GOTTLIEB)

This is the house of the living.
People stand in these rooms and talk
about things that happened to them.
Enslavement things.

For a plantation house it's a tiny place
in a speck of time, a few rooms
collapsed with partitions.
So bare, so crowded.
Some want to burn it down;
some want to treasure it.
Will the ghosts welcome the patronage
of visitors? Caretakers of their own
Ghostly Hosting Service
for the watching and curious?

To the Ones Who Never Left the Plantation

(WITH DANIEL BOATNER V.)

If I never leave this plantation tell the others
I lived.
Tell them I went from the porch to the garden
walking with my good
shoes on my broad feet, my mind tight
and aware.
Don't let them talk about me the way they talk
about the lost fox
who died underneath some broken branch,
beaten and unknown.
If I never leave this plantation know my voice
traveled, smooth,
and recollecting speeches of unity and love—
I am man unburdened
and human.
Yes, some of Us never leave this place,
we never went
into town or hooked our arms around the shoulder
of a beautiful woman.
We never rode on the back of a rickety wagon
or smelled the grass
of a city lawn. But I survived and had a name,
call me not
easily undone.

A My People Poem

(WITH DORIS MCLEOD-WILLIAMS)

You heard from the crack of the door.
You turned the crystal knob
only to have it shut at the tip of your nose.
You were little and ran fast and listened
enough to catch up to the goings and comings.

Now we piece together the people—
White, Black, and Multiracial.
We are relatives, seekers of a more peaceful
Revolution than what created our genealogy.

I want to know what you know about my people,
I said to the caretaker's granddaughter.
I want you to tell me something about them.
How about the way their fingers curled in the air?
Or the way they played a game while
others slept quietly in their comfortable beds?
Did my great-grandfather know that he was enslaved?
The voice of my mother when she held
your babies tight to the milk of her chest—
Did she cuddle your babies
the way she should have cuddled
her daydreams into existence?
I want to know what you know about my people.
Who were you to know this about them?
We are ready to scream the part that once was whispered.

By My Own Eyes

(WITH DORIS MCLEOD-WILLIAMS)

"Feels like the oven is on," Mama would say
about September in Alabama

Dander from the trees
at my grandfather's grave

where I cried so good
and I traced this headstone with my knuckles

I never thought I would see the day

A Black cemetery in the back, on a floor of pinecones
along a makeshift road and a locked gate
The dead endured

their unmarked graves

Will the earth pick me up if I fall
If my knees land in the dusty shirt pocket of my grandfather's
remains
will I get back up again

Will the earth stay calm while I scream
the names of the ones not wanting to come back

settle into the morning's damp rise
The saints around my grandfather's grave, they march.

I Make Headstones of my Lovers

(WITH DORIS MCLEOD-WILLIAMS)

Where enslaved persons are buried—
no headstones.
There would be, could be, twenty-two
but I will count by two:
Two were my age, and the ones consented to.
Two held my hand and looked into my eyes.
Two recognized my beauty.
Twenty took me to the cemetery for the first time.
I laid my fully clothed body on the places
where headstones should be.
I laid down in reverence to my younger selves,
I laid the wreaths over their dead necks.
I traced my finger on the sky.

Wreath Laying a Goodbye

(WITH HENRY SMITH)

I shall see you again
But today I see you in the clouds
that write your name, son of mine,
notched next to an enslaved Grandfather

I shall remember from
the grief of fatherhood that speaks
cold and coddled
In the memory of a son buried
behind a cotton field

Glory in the remembering
Lay a wreath for kinship
Call forth the pastoral fields to sing
Witness that somebody was born, birthed
and sweated back to the earth

I shall count the number of days
that you were loved and
I will place a flower around
the rings of my heart,
too numerous to unchain

I shall see you again
In the cemetery where you are
next to the family of resistance
where I lay this wreath
The sweet slaves, the sweet chariots,
took home some daughters, some sons, some too early

Releasing What We Should at the Cemetery

(WITH NELL GOTTLIEB)

Call out their names and see them
as stardust in clouds of rain.
We cut the locks so our loved ones could fly.

We turn our eyes away from the statues
of our white man's heritage.

Take us to the marbled sandstone where
Black grandmothers and grandfathers rest, finally.

I Do Descend

(WITH JULIA COTLAR)

My great-great-great-grandfather used
a wagon trail for slave trade
if I'd been inside that wagon
safe and protected
I'd have eaten from the plate
of a white woman
while my family's migration set
the course to kill
the freedom of other families

I was the girl who visited plantations
not knowing
that my molecular makeup was *plantation,*
I too descended
from the ones who lashed their demands
and I too descended
from the ones who built
a world for whiteness to celebrate
without whiteness earning its keep
Cousins who call me cousin when
we hug at Homecomings
I tell them that I am a Wallace too

Prelude to a Sweeter Belonging

(WITH HENRY SMITH)

So for the slave, Death, was a sweet day?
No more sadness, no more pitiful plowing
Reuniting with one's own self
Kissing the ones so dearly missed, so dearly departed
So for the slave, Death, indeed was a sweet day
When death touched the Black man's soul,
Oh, how dignified and how far and free
the bird with clipped wing flies
Fly away from thee!

What I Didn't Expect in Harpersville

(WITH DANIEL BOATNER V.)

Upon arrival
I found people, my people
Black, proud people
I found land, my land
land drizzled in honeycomb-syrup
I found a grandmother crying
on the grave of her grandfather,
a large headstone sculpted
from the hands of the enslaved
I learned the front porch stories
At the Black folks' cemetery
I read aloud to the dead and buried
while I stood with white and Black relatives
And we circled around in the dirt

Coming to Alabama taught me
to be solemn and wild
Stepping onto slave land as they called it,
the heat stirred up my ancestors' rivers
I came across a self I didn't expect I could become
and siblings who raised food in farmland
broken by cotton gins
the speckle of God's grace left in Alabama
calling each other kin
those who risk coming home,
who narrate the reclaimed
land and find healing.

Gonna Be A Tourist Stop

There are worse things, I suppose,
than marking a plantation house
as a historic thing and fashioning
a tourist stop. But it won't suit
reconciliation if it's refurbished
to nestle in suburbia.

The Woman *in the* Yellow Apron

Heritage

the woman in the yellow apron
is my great-grandmother and
yellow daughter had a daddy father
and a mother
sisters and brothers
family and yellow was dreamed about
and dreamed into existence

Spoiling the Spoiled

(WITH BEVERLY JOHNSON)

My sister said
at the roots
I was spoiled
all my life
because my mama
always did my hair
I never learned
how to braid or part
straight the line
I never learned
how to grease
my scalp or keep
my edges slick
I only remember
my mother's hands
in my head-
my curly hair
and I think how
Black folks spoil
the spoiled,
love the spoiled
so when mama
started to pass away
I bent down
next to her, looking
deep into her crown,
the corners of her cornrows,
straight and always laid

though I never
learned how to braid
I never
learned how
to grease my scalp
I wish for
my mother's hands
hugging the strands
of my crown again
recoiling the coil
of spoiling the spoiled.

This Apron Was Made with Love and Aspiration

Sometimes it's all I got
Yellow apron
Large belly
Round
I eat my share
You know
You better
Not go hungry
You Better
if you want to live

Being alive is tree sap and sunlight too
One day this yellow apron
will be left upstairs
on the mattress
sunk and shapeless
Today it's around my neck
snug to my waist
full of the crumbs
this earth provided

To Black Girls Who Love Birds

(WITH ANGIE ODEN)

Mornings, I wake early
before the world shrinks
my smile.
I rest my arms on the windowsill
so I can feel the humming and the chorus—
the kingdom of birds.

Black girls are not supposed to
love birds so much.
Not the Alabama Yellowhammer
nor Swallow-tailed Kite.
Not the chipping Sparrow.
Black birds swarm in flight.

What the songbird knows,
the people in this sleeping town
fear. A dark and widowed land
where everyone who isn't a bird
flies everywhere and nowhere at all.
Black girls are not supposed to love birds,
but so much I crave
the summering bluebirds
to witness every dream.

Know and Remember, Blood Stories Retold

(WITH NELL GOTTLIEB)

In a town where everyone knows everyone
I listened and watched
Whenever my great-grandmother talked
I spotted the red bird behind her back
I saw the ancestors finding their way back
into the heirloom of ascension
as she whistled wisdom
and connected her stories to mine

The dent of my bottom on my grandmother's sofa
Blue hot history scrubbed with mountain and wind
Black folks learn history, soupy and sour
from the couches of elders
Anticipation stories
Emancipation stories
And what remains:
The down and down and on and on
of praise, reviving time in elegies

The Other Revival is Coming

Not giving herself wholesale to white people
who thought they'd be getting all of her

Underneath her costume, she's a genius
and no one gets to see her beauty

She looks like a domestic person
who works for a truer spirit

The Air Upstairs at the Wallace House Has a Perfume of Saving Grace

The Ancestors want me to write to them,
not about them.
To write the silhouette of their bodies
back into form.
A Black mother lives upstairs and she
is disturbed.
Her body is shapeless. She is water dancing
and the walls stain her
with shadows—
Every move from one room to the next, restless.
I worry about her
every time I walk the house. I dare tell
what she speaks.
I translate her from scents.

The Woman in the Yellow Apron, A Seer

At the altar of Mother Ancestor
there is a holy supper,
Sweet and sacred and everlasting.
At the altar of Mother Ancestor
there is a passing of time that feels
slow and quiet.
At the altar of Mother Ancestor
there is a longing to seek and to be seen
raw and unflinching.
At the altar of Mother Ancestor
a fellowship is yet to be revealed
in history books or archived at the hands of man.
There is sunshine in cheeks
curiosity without fear
a potent reckoning
spring water for a daughter's thirst
a haunting we found to be a kind of home.

The Woman in the Yellow Apron as Medicine

The Medicine Mother is a balm to the land. Overseer of acres for
generations.
Mother Ancestor can predict rain from clouds hovering.
She says when the cows lay down, tucking tails between their legs,
a storm is brewing. Then, she takes out her silver tinctures and
collects rain
water in drops, to treat the people who cry. She transforms this
house into
a hospice for those who worked while gales tore through.
The tinctures lined the back porches of the Wallace House,
awaiting the men folks to come for their healing.

Touch is her medicine.
The men with oil on their
foreheads rest underneath
oak and mulberry trees
next to the children's buried pottery.

The woods will come alive again with howls.
The animals will roar
and awaken their unmerciful masters.

Tasting Life on Plantation Pure

White people swarming sweetly at parties
inside a house that smells of cottonwood and danger

Tasting honey straight from the comb
of the honeybee

The yellow apron'd woman
carries sweetness drizzled

in a clean glass jar
Her breath rolls through the hunger

As guests take the honey from her
while she, the one who bakes and serves,

dreams yellow until it's clear enough to see through.

The Woman
in the Yellow
Apron Departs
for a Tent
Revival

A New American South: Impressions from the Front Porch on Juneteenth

When the South says *revival*
does it mean Black homecomings and
voices so loud and proud that they break
the chained resistance of the enslaved horror?
When the South says *revival*
does revolution find its way?
Black cookouts are Camelot
in the South—
Celebrations despite
the forked tongues that pressed cruelty
when the South said *survival*,
instead of *reparation*.

Good Things the Dead Leave Behind

(WITH ANGIE ODEN)

Before death steals joy
I will remind my family
of courage

Before the Revival
came a revolt when
fire burned our oak trees

Before canvas blocked the sun
We were trusting and steady
when the world let go

Before my family—
dusk and dawn-strong
in the afterglow.

Ye Olde Revival

Maybe if the church needed a new roof, or if the people didn't have a building to worship in, the pastor would call for a revival.

Or if the pastor needed to pay for church things or send the first lady (pastor wife) away on some kind of respite, he'd call for a revival.

People with tiny bibles and less love in their hearts would leave the plantation and walk to the tent. The revival took place in some empty field or on a dirt road close to the Coosa River.

Baptizing took place on the first Sundays.When the water was warm, those bodies would go under cold and burst up as hot flesh swollen for the journey eternal.

Poets Always Speak in Tongues

I start to interrupt, to ask permission
and then I fall to my knees, asking to speak

When we repair our ties to the Mother Ancestor
we suffer grief

This revival is finishing the sentences
of those swallowed whole, complete...

At the Coosa

I found my own religion—the remembering of who I am
Reborn
At the Coosa River
A tent revival
At the Coosa River
I reclaimed my Grandmothers' and Grandfathers' condition
A river of faith
At the Coosa River
I laid down the burdens of distress
A twelfth generation
At the Coosa River
my haunted feet danced beautiful
At the Coosa River
revival found me
Put breath back
into my body
naming me Mother Ancestor
A whole woman, a whole humanity
I caught the spirit in fields of grace, thankfulness, forgiveness
Dear Mother Ancestor
the Other Revival awaits.

Turn

(WITH HYDEIA AVERETT)

Grandmother would say that real faith will set
a soul on fire.
Burn down a witch's curse and cause
people to leave
this place. Wrap the insides of evil here.
Sink their ankles into
a damp so dense
bodies turn blood orange.
Faith sets a soul on fire—a siren for the Pastor
to preach. The world is burning
and this time it is for real.

Patchwork Blues, Stitched Time

(WITH HYDEIA AVERETT)

This is somebody's home.
These shingled roofs are stories
woven cleverly
over generations of porches
hosting singers and tellers—
somebody is home,
tapping their toes on loose floor planks.
Smooth voices caress the air.
Somebody is here, sewing the blue.

Let Me Bid You an Altar

(WITH ANGIE ODEN)

Freedom, a ripe sweet cherry in the middle of a sour day.
Freedom, jumping Double Dutch on the sidewalk of the church
grounds.
Freedom, New Year's fireworks behind the old tire shop.

The skin of freedom glistens and hastens
a body to unchain and become.

Living among the weeds, those mothers who left
us proud, even in that harvest.

Smells Like Rain

(WITH ANGIE ODEN)

Drought won't last long this time
The drought won't last long this time
How do I know?
Cause we can feel the sweet smell of rain
Long gone
Long gone
Drought won't last long this time
Mama said
She knows because her bones stretched thin
come back to life
Stretched thinner than the blood
of the skeleton remains
Mama said
Drought won't last long this time
'cause we can feel the sweet smell of rain
dripping down way deep
Mama said.

Sisters Remember on the Front Porch of the Wallace Plantation

(WITH MARY AND CYNTHIA DATCHER, SISTERS)

*Black people grow up with these stories, so we hear what happened to our
ancestors, we hear them told over and over and over again.
These stories seep into bones.*

Deep in rural places, old-fashioned tent revivals pop up in the
woods and in the hot grounds of fields and cement parking lots.
The white tents fold people into their shade, hosting multitudes
of church folks looking to get religious. Revive us again spills out,
along with the rapid sprint of Amens.

Tent preachers have a lot to say to the people. The listeners sit,
sweaty and sultry in their seats, holding bibles and advising each
other about how good God is.

But there is another revival that takes place on front porches and
on corner lots, away from the big tents. When the lights go dim
and the outdoor candle burns, Black elders testify about who they
belong to and who belongs to them. This is history keeping.

Sometimes, in Alabama, we are not allowed to teach our history in
educational spaces. But we still keep history. The history keepers
erect tents of their own: on doorsteps, in circles of folding chairs,
at the tables we prop up. Hummingbirds gather to mourn with us
when our stories are filled with longing.

These new tent revivals, built by artists, poets, and cultural
workers, and peacemakers, are creative and bountiful. These
are the family of folks who cook, dance, and turn the porches

into pews. The new tent revival is not there so people can catch fire. Its purpose is to cool the embers of battlegrounds, settling the rattling from the brittle quake of earth's harm. Bear witness to what happens when the shaking stops and dreams moss the layers of where we find faith. The porch revival is a space of Black regulation where the nervous system is calmed and regulated. This revival returns us back to who we are and have always known ourselves to be—African, Beautiful, Human, Awakened, Reimagined, Rural, Love.

Road *to the* History House

The Road to History House

This is a different journey.
I tuck my apron into the root cellar
and walk away from Wallace House.
Could be three country miles or three hundred
to Peter Datcher's house
over in Creswell.

I see him under his brimmed cap
and he's sitting on the porch.
He encourages everybody into him.
The house is a mess one lady says.
A hoarding disorder says her husband.
That's the real history I say.

Creswell: A Severe Need for Joy

(WITH HYDEIA AVERETT AND PETER DATCHER)

In Creswell
Black landowners own the land
and reclaim their livelihood

the severe need for joy
of this sacred place
where humidity is a prolonged fever

and the heart sutures two kingdoms
one where the farmland is rich
And another sparse

Flimsy stems daring to hold on
Creswell a wishing flower
Fragile and radical

between courage and sweetness
is a small country road town
where talk is communion—
a new revival.

Our House, Made After the Wallace Plantation House

(WITH PETER DATCHER)

See, they expect us to have no joy.
But in our house we practice
joy each day
by whispering I love you to our souls.
                                See they expect us
to have no joy.
We were made
to thrive but we choose
that strange, undying devotion.
To live and not die.

Made in Rural Alabama

(WITH HYDEIA AVERETT)

Mrs. Mary Lee talks about racism all the time.
Blue black racism.
Racism that has folks standing in long lines.
Blue black racism in the back of restaurants.
Racism that kept her body revolving around a hot sun.
Pricked-blood-red-fingertips-turning-cotton-into-brillow-sacks-
that-read-Made-in-Alabama racism.
Mrs. Mary Lee don't take no junk though.
Racism can't stop her from praising,
Mrs. Mary Lee: Don't take any junk.
Her spirit is an eagle's wing.
Mrs. Mary Lee knows about racism.
Her mouth was raw with truth.
Mrs. Mary Lee isn't about taking no junk.
Her courage led to a revolution.
Made in rural Alabama where her people
Don't take no junk.

Don't take no junk.

Black Womanhood a Homecoming

(WITH PETER DATCHER)

In fact Black women had it worse than men as the enslaved cook, wet nurse, cotton picker, and night nurse to the master, having to work hard in the house, in the fields, and without their consent on their backs—

Black women have been holding a collective breath for 400 years. We release.

So, why can't we just return, why can't we just get back to our homes, why can't we find our own way back to ourselves. Why must the journey be such of a refrain, a monotone testimony, such a slow walk?

Why must the journey be such of a refrain, a monotone testimony, such a slow walk?

Because we must witness

We must walk alongside the othered and the withering we must bring them along with us and

We must be willing to wander with undying curiosity and never fret about the veering off

We must lay concrete for sidewalks and level the streets we must become traffic lights and transport the weary and the lost

We must put the woman with bags and oversized purses on our backs we must provide swaddle cloth for the babies and straighten the crooked lines in the road

This journey isn't one for the faint however on this journey there will be dancing, and spraying purple dye in our hair and skirts

that sweep beneath our knees and there would be lots of joy,
laughter that flies to the cemetery of the buried

Dinner will be served hot, large pots of soups and stew and rice
and gravy, the women shall bake and beat dough for biscuits
and brew morning strength as days are long and naps are the
mainstay, years and years of napping.

But we must first be a witness, and we must finally bear witness...

Witnessing the widening of the circle and making more room
for the culture of sisters to be seen, to be heard, to be felt, to BE
gathered together, This is the Homecoming of Black Womanhood.

Revived and Replenished.

The Archivist

It ain't the fancy degree
or the showboat of professors
what some call scholars
to digitize and professionalize
what Peter already knows how to do:
keep the pictures taped on the walls,
and gather folks for stories.
The tintypes he gave to the library,
that he gave away for free,
he forgives himself for giving
even though other people
are so upset but he forgives himself.

He started by keeping his mother's promises
to remember certain things.

A keeper museum like his
cherishes and collects our heritage.
Everyone wants to come to his house
because it is alive. There's nothing dead in there.
The fading nature of the pictures
which I think allows visitors to get closer
in the keepers history that do not look like the people
in the pages of the books,
while three miles off, the Wallace house is swept clean.

The Peter Datcher Poem Cycle

(WITH PETER DATCHER)

I.

In the Beginning.

In the beginning there was the life of the enslaved man and the enslaved woman fully evolved, fully loved, fully remembered. The culture was rich with exploration of self, culture, and environment.

Love arose from the overflow and became a symphony. Black folks lit lanterns for love, cooked beans for strength, beat drums to say what they needed to say, quilted garments for warmth. Come and breathe in this testimony of the many ways God answers prayer. Come and breathe.

II.

Today, Now and Forevermore.

Come inside and see the many faces proud with laughter. Imagine the batches of soup prepared to cure and heal the waiting throats of friends and guests. Watch how the torn fragments of a society are put back together again as Black folks center their lives as whole.

The preacher raises his voice. He shouts so the pews won't remain cold from one white man's gaze. Feel the presence of liberated people. Go deeper. Deepen into the knowing of one another. Eat from the farm of the forefathers where the crops of suffering are fresh with prominence. Come and breathe.

III.

Benediction.

History is the balm that rubs forgiveness whole. History
found and revealed me, causing me to spark a revolution.
History called my name and set my feet on solid ground. In
my grandmother's house are many memories of the ways we
lived and thrived. The sadness sits on tables and inside the
worn stapled books. I nearly died watching the roof leak.
I felt the tears of women who worked harder than men. This
is how we put up the tent in the wind and the rain. We paved
our own fort and forged our own revolution. We are what
remains and what was revived. We survive.

The Other Revival Poem #1

When the others died
The woman in the yellow apron
Took to her bed
Resting her eyes away from an outside sorrow
The doors locked from the inside
She wrapped herself in pessimism
Throwing quilts over her Virginia body
Lukewarm from the distance of home
Grief softened her
The suffering stretched her straight
Bravery a visitation
Fear turned toward the wayward land
Hope climbed in bed with the mother
No longer emptiness
Musings of the eternal.

Words From Descendants of the Wallace House Plantation

1819: Letter from the Ancestors to the Living Descendants of the Wallace House from the Africa of My Lips-Sip

(WITH BLACK DESCENDANTS)

Dear Family,

You may be reading about me and the rest of us. We lived in Alabama and were enslaved on the Wallace Plantation. This is our letter to each one of you. We weren't allowed to discuss such things. Today, we write this letter to show that we lived. In fact, we are plain in spirit and clothing, but we soar. We are ready to witness and listen.

> When the drums begin to beat,
> when the air falls silent
> When the south clenches us,
> sip from the Africa of my lips,
> dip your finger into the overflow of my deep,
> bare the ease of this beauty
> Rest in compassion
>
> Breathe as if you are taking your last
> Wipe the dust from the bottom of your feet
> Breathe
> Crawl inside the rib cage of the Africa of your Ancestors
> And Breathe

Sincerely,
The Ancestors

"Do you know what the largest plantation is? It is Shelby County. There was a plantation almost as large as this one. I found it by accident when I was looking for the largest plantations in the county.

[There were] 80 slaves. It had almost 45 kids two to three years old, and others between 45 and 65—no way they possibly had those children themselves. We buy them and take them out. Slavery wasn't all about people, it was about money.

The slave trade—it did not want to be transporting babies, so they would be sold and would never know who mom and dad were, never know if there family was alive. Mothers never seeing their children again. This is what our people went through right here in Shelby County and I'm shutting up with that said—not another word. Dirt can run over the mountain before a slave mother could see her child again, that's what happened right here."

"After my mother passed, I went to going through things, and one day I was out here and I was going in the trunks, and I went to seeing all these pictures and documents, and my mother had kept all this stuff, when I went to looking at everything, I said, oh my God, I said. Well, nobody living in here.

I'm gonna put these things up, I'm gonna put these pictures, when people come here, they get to see."

— *Peter Datcher: Black Descendant, June 17, 2023. Juneteenth Celebration at Wallace House with all Black Descendants in attendance*

"I was always interested in the history of Alabama, and it was fed down my throat. I was brought up hearing about the "Lost Cause." The complexity of it, in one way, escaped me, and in another way, it didn't, because I went on to graduate school in sociology. I spent the whole semester of my freshman year trying to figure out the apartheid nation that I was actually living in. I had never questioned the order of things.

...What really changed for me was in 2012 during my high school reunion. I went to Ramsay. I started asking people what they knew about the Civil Rights Movement. They knew so little, and shocking and strange as it was, it was true. That set me off. I retired in 2011 and went to art school in Houston. I started doing work based on imagery through Birmingham. And then I got a lot of feedback that I was appropriating Black pain. So in 2018, I thought about what I really knew.

That was the same year my cousin called about the house, and he said he wanted me to have it. I finally agreed to take the house after several years of saying no. It was a litany of woes, but I knew I wanted to do something with this."

— *Nell Gottleib: White Descendant, October 7, 2023*

"I remember Anderson Wallace, my grandfather and his hair, it was like cotton—so soft, so gray, I can remember his hair until this day.

I can't [help] thinking about slaves—slave women and all how they did their hair. When you see pictures you see such beautiful hair, like slave women had the most beautiful hair. I wonder what they did, was it some kind of homemade oils or plants? But their hair was so beautiful.

It was at the roots.

Before my mamma died last year, she was the descendant of this Wallace house. She would still do my hair as a grown woman right up until she passed away. My sister said I was spoiled all my life because my mamma always did my hair. I never had to worry about it. That's what I miss—my mamma doing my hair. She had beautiful hair and growing hands."

— *Beverly Johnson: Black Descendant, June 19, 2023. Descendants' Day*

"My grandmother on my father's side had her children later in life. She worked as a free woman at the Wallace house. My grandfather worked there as a slave. Everybody in my family said that when I was little—my grandmother from the Wallace side—said I was going to be a school teacher. She said that I was so smart and she just knew that I was going to be a teacher. My uncles and everybody call me 'School Teacher.' I think that was my grandmother Wallace's dream or goal, I don't know.

One thing about the Black descendants [of] this generation is doing their thing with life and have superseded what my grandmother and grandfather went through… I can't [help] but wonder how they lived their life and who they could have become. Who we all could have been."

— *Candi McGinnis: Black Descendant, June 28, 2023*

"When I had a question to my cousin Peter Datcher about [the] Wallaces... Peter couldn't answer my question. Peter said, 'Well, let me put you in contact with Nell.' That was when I heard about my great-grandfather, Robert Wallace. In my conversation I had with Nell in 2018 she asked me if the name Homer meant anything to me. I said he was one of my Grandma's oldest brothers. She stated that she played with Homer as a child but he was much older than her. I found that to be most interesting since I only knew his name and she knew him and had interactions with him personally. I knew then I had to stay in touch with her. I love her and have great admiration for her."

"And Nell said to me, 'Maybe I can fill in the void.' ... And it gave me a sense of, I AM BECAUSE OF MY ANCESTORS that I never knew. I wished I was able to connect with them."

—*Doris McLeod-Williams: Black Descendant, Oct 7, 2023. Homecoming.*

"We were brought up in love, so that is the basis for everything we do… and that's what you do, most Black families, that's what they do, and you hope that's what they do, because you realize—hey, you get a whole bunch of ancestors who went through a lot of crap just so you could be here. So. You need to really show yourself as being someone who could carry that going forward, and you can make yourself look like—okay, this is beautiful. I'm gonna do the best that I can, that my ancestors have done and do even better, because I know what they went through.

Black people grow up with these stories, so we hear what happened to our ancestors, we hear them told over and over and over again. So, we need to have this put down… That's like, I believe the healing can occur, and so hearing these stories growing up and then coming here and actually seeing, this is it.. It's something that seeps into your bones, and you go, this is like a full circle memory…

Now our ancestors, I hope, are going, yes, thank you, thank you, thank you, and exhaling in their graves and say now, hopefully all the hard work, the pain that we've gone through, hopefully now you can share with others, and this will, moving forward, make other people realize that, this country has a scar that needs to be healed… but we can heal it, and we're doing that by doing this.

And so for me, it's just coming full circle and saying, yes, this is bring[ing] me back to my history, back to my roots, because it's always there, it never leaves you, so you can go off and do as many things as you want, I've done quite a few things in my lifetime, but this history never leaves."

— *Mary and Cynthia Datcher: Black Descendants, October 7, 2023. Homecoming.*

Laying of the Wreath in memory of loved ones.

"We lay this wreath for all slaves that are buried here in Wallace Cemetery. They are unknown to us because when they died, no one thought enough to put a marker or anything on the grave, although they are known to us, they are unknown to our Lord and Savior.

He knew each and every one of them by name. Even knowing the number of hairs on their head, since they are unknown to us, I'm gonna talk about something we knew about them, and that is their life. They work from sunrise to sunset. Day after day, week after week, month after month. Year after year. They never received a check, a salary. They could never take a sick day. They never accumulated vacation time. They live with the threat each and every day that their family could be divided. Fathers could be sold from the mother and children. The brother could be sold from sisters.

They lived this life. Cotton fields surrounding a sour memory, a sore to the flesh, a thorn to the side. Buried across the road from cotton and king south's most miserable memory."

—*Henry Wallace Smith: October 7, 2023. Homecoming.*

(This interview took place as Henry laid a wreath at the cemetery of enslaved descendants where his son is buried. He is one of the oldest living Black elder descendants of the Wallace family known in the area of Harpersville.)

Naming a Flower

(WITH HYDEIA AVERETT)

Hydeia, whose name sounds and reads like a flower, reminisces about her 83-year-old grandmother's toughness and how she didn't allow her spirit to be broken by white people's unfairness. She is part of the closely woven Creswell community, knitted together in Harpersville through her grandmother.

Hydeia speaks to the pride of Black American life in rural Alabama and the importance of land, family, and the pattern of revival that exists when perseverance is the spirit of resistance.

"My Grandmother, she helped cook and knit and quilt with his mom, with Mr. Peter's mom, on the same porch of the History House. [And she] passed down a quilt to all of her grand girls... The one that she originally gave me, I lost in the house fire.

But the ones that she still has, they all, they all have these different patterns, all these different patterns to form and make a bigger picture. It's just like she said, that they would grab different pieces of fabric from anything or anywhere and kind of form it together.

So to me, it's just taking, simply taking, what you have and making something out of nothing, um, and, and putting it, putting it to use is simply... Anything you can make anything out of nothing as long as, you know, put the work in and actually try.

I went to school, um, in Birmingham, and, and I took some pictures of my son in the cotton field. And most people [said], 'Why are you allowing him to take a picture in a cotton field?'

But to me, it's different, because this is home, and not only is it home, but it's home [that is] grown by a family or by a surrounding family. So I see it as pride—like, I take pride in. And what we see, not necessarily disappointment, because it did exist, but just to see how far we come.

— *Hydeia Averett: Black Descendant, March 17, 2024*

"My grandmother tells the story about all the time that she would have us sit down and read books... it was more so her teaching us that there was more to life than just fun, you know, you had to learn... Reading was fun to her because we weren't allowed to write. She didn't know how to write, so being able to write was just a blessing in general back then, so, us being able to read freely, to her, was like... look, in my day, my mother and I, she didn't really get to do this. I want you guys to do things I wasn't able to do as a child... Kids not gonna understand why they shouldn't be acting like that, like a way, unless you give them an example, you give them a story. She had all the story."

— *Daniel Boater V: Black Descendant, October 7, 2023*

"This is personal. How do you love something that is flawed.

How do you reconcile your own experiences with what you know
is truth,
For me, I feel healing right is small,
Deeply rooted reasons. Deeply rooted.
I see the urgency there (Harpersville) and I see that there is a lot
of work to be done."

–*Julia Cotlar: White Descendant, October 7, 2023*

"My mother talked a lot about how her father was a slave here at the Wallace house. That's what everyone calls it, 'the Wallace house,' and how next to the house — which is now a tire shop or something—[there] used to be a little house that they wished they could play on. She said it felt like freedom to play in the fields and around that house.

So many things about that house and having a great-grandfather who worked as a slave and built the house makes me wonder how he and my grandmother met, and had to work, and found peace in nature. Maybe there was some peace for my great-grandmother.

I don't have a picture of her, but we have some of Anderson Wallace, and he was very handsome. I wonder if he felt like the Wallace house was his home. Even if it was good, it wasn't good if you know what I mean. But this house was their home or place they lived.

I want my great-grandfather to be remembered as a spirit who lived who built a foundation and was a handsome good man. Now we are to be remembered as a successful family who reclaimed this land and this house as our own no matter how much control we have here and thrived on the land as our own."

—*Angie Oden: Black Descendant, June 19, 2023*

"I have one word, healing. That's my hope—is to heal this family, heal all families, and heal the nation of this scourge. I think that's happening today."

—*Donna Wallace Carson, Black Descendant, October 7, 2023. Homecoming*

Biographies of Harpersville Descendants

HYDEIA AVERITT
Hydeia is a mother and actress in Alabama. She graduated from
the Historical Black College, Miles College with a Bachelor's in
Fine Arts. Hydeia found her love for acting with her beloved
grandmother while watching television as a young child. Hydeia
is a descendant of the Wallaces and resides in rural Shelby County
Alabama on her family's land.

DANIEL BOATNER V.
Daniel is the grandson of Doris McLeod-Williams. He is a sixth
grade teacher, artist, and creator in Detroit, Michigan. At
twenty-six, Daniel is a part of the youngest Wallace Descendant
generation and he attended, and contended, with his Wallace
history and the Wallace House plantation's storied legacy. Daniel
grew up with family stories of his enslaved and enslavers
descendants from his grandmother. He is the second great-
grandson of Luddie Wallace and Frank Kidd, the third great-
grandson of Bob Wallace and Ann Callie Cohill, and his fourth
great-grandparents were Henry Wallace and Phoebe Wallace.

DONNA WALLACE CARSON

Donna is an educator from Chicago, Illinois where she and her husband started a nonprofit for Black urban youth on boat and water safety. Donna came to Harpersville Wallace House Homecoming for the first time in 2023 with her husband Gilbert Carson. Donna heard about family stories from her relatives and is a descendant of Anderson Wallace of the Wallace House Plantation.

JULIA COTLAR

Julia is a descendant of Sam Wallace through Nell Wallace Gottlib. She is a nineteen-year-old Jewish white American, who lives in Austin, Texas, and who attended the University of California, Berkeley. She studied nuclear engineering with a minor in public policy. Julia has attended Homecomings since 2018.

ALBERT "PETER" DATCHER

Albert "Peter" Datcher (Uncle Pete) is a farmer and family historian in the Cresswell Community outside Harpersville. Datcher is descended from Lucy Wallace Baker, who was enslaved on the Wallace Plantation, and who, after emancipation, was the first of three generations of midwives. It was Datcher's once-enslaved great-grandfather who purchased the first hundred acres of land that his family continues to farm—land that was formerly part of a plantation. Since it was purchased after the Civil War, the farm has grown to nearly four hundred acres, quadrupling in size. A member of the Board of the Shelby County Historical Society, Peter Datcher has placed historic and contemporary photographs and articles on every wall of his ancestral home, now known as the Datcher History House. Datcher's display includes more than a century's collection of mementos, photographs, and documents that tell the story of his family's journey from enslavement to freedom to becoming successful farmers. Along the way, there are stories of triumph and tragedy, of hard times and family celebrations. Family relics, such as Lucy Wallace Baker's uniform, tools, and records are in the collection of the Alabama History Museum.

Peter Datcher's biography was sourced with information from This is Alabama

MARY DATCHER

Mary Datcher is a media, branding, and political consultant in Chicago. She is Vice President of Communications for APS & Associates, a public affairs and political consulting firm. She was formerly District Director for Illinois Congressman Bobby Rush (retired) and Congressman Jonathan L. Jackson. She was a former senior staff writer/arts & entertainment editor for *The Chicago Defender*. Datcher's father left Harpersville during the Great Migration and relocated to Chicago. She is a descendant of Lucy Wallace Baker, who was enslaved at the Wallace Plantation.

CYNTHIA DATCHER

Cynthia Datcher is an actress from Chicago, Illinois. She has nearly 40 television and film credits to her name and starred in *Goode Behavior* (1996–1997) and *18 Wheels Of Justice* (2000–2001). She is the sister of Mary Datcher, who sits on the board of the Wallace Center for Arts and Reconciliation and is the cousin of Peter Datcher who sits on the board as well. Datcher's father left Harpersville during the Great Migration and relocated to Chicago. She is a descendant of Lucy Wallace Baker, who was enslaved at the Wallace Plantation.

NELL WALLACE HARRELL GOTTLIEB

The cofounder of the Wallace Center for Arts and Reconciliation, Nell was born in Birmingham Alabama, and moved away in 1962. She spent summers in the 1950s at the Wallace House with her grandmother. She was the second great-granddaughter of Samuel Wallace (1784–1869), great-granddaughter of Wales Wellington Wallace (1832–1901), and the granddaughter of Samuel Henderson Wallace (1880–1947). Gottlieb inherited the house in 2018 and gifted it to Klein Arts & Culture in 2019. In 2023, the nonprofit's name was changed to the Wallace Center for Arts and Reconciliation. A graduate of Emory University and Boston University, she was a professor of public health education at the University of Texas at Austin from 1980 to 2011. Upon retirement, she attended the Glassell School of Art and is now an artist.

BEVERLY ODEN JOHNSON

Beverly Oden Johnson, a retired nurse, has been an elected member of the Harpersville Town Council for over sixteen years. She is descended from Anderson Wallace, who was enslaved on the Wallace Plantation. She lives in Harpersville and her family has a long lineage with the Wallace Center for Arts and Reconciliation as a board member.

CANDI MCGINNIS POSEY

McGinnis is a teacher in Alabama and has always felt that education and teaching is her calling. She is a proud graduate of the University of Montevallo in Shelby County, Alabama which is close to her Harpersville upbringing. She is the great-granddaughter of Wallace descendants. McGinnis's great-grandmother and great-grandfather are descendants of the Wallace House and the McGinnis's are known for the work they contributed to the Wallace House and Wallace family. Her great-grandmother worked as a freed slave on the plantation and her great-grandfather worked in the house as a person who was enslaved.

ANGIE ODEN

Angie's great-grandfather is Anderson Wallace, a direct descendant of enslavement of the Wallace plantation. Angie's mother passed down stories of the Wallaces to her and her sisters. Angie finds joy working in Harpersville during Homecoming and special events where she is able to connect her story with Black and white descendants of the Wallace House. Angie resides in Birmingham, Alabama and works in technology and customer relations. On the project, she said, "I will remind my family of the clipping from newspapers that speak of courage in the History House so we wouldn't get discouraged. Peter's History House, my mother said, was full of writings that stated that our folks didn't die or couldn't be forgotten. We must remember and be remembered."

HENRY SMITH

A retired teacher and coach, Smith is a descendant of Anderson Wallace, who was enslaved at the Wallace plantation. Henry's beloved son is buried at the African-American cemetery where he lays a wreath annually for Wallace House homecomings and contributes to the upkeep of the cemetery. An Elder Wallace Descendant, Henry is one of the oldest known living Black descendants of the Wallace family in the area of Harpersville.

DORIS MCLEOD-WILLIAMS

Mrs. Doris McLeod is the matriarch of the family's historical narrative. She resides in Michigan. McLeod has been keeping her family's descendant record for over 20 years. Her precise record keeping has contributed to the Datcher History House collections and the correct archival information of the Wallace record. She is a descendant of Henry and Phoebe Wallace, Luddie Wallace and Frank Kidd, Bob Wallace and Ann Callie Cohill.

THEOANGELO (THEO) PERKINS

Cofounder of the Wallace Center for Arts and Reconciliation, Theoangelo (Theo) Perkins is now in a fourth-term as Mayor of Harpersville. He is a former teacher, a realtor, and a minister. His grandmother worked at the Wallace House as a maid and caregiver for children. His McGinnis ancestors came to the Wallace farm after emancipation and have been connected with the Wallaces over generations.

Acknowledgments

Community serves as my sails and as the waters that helped shape this book. I am grateful to the descendant community in Harpersville, Alabama. The descendants of the Wallace House Plantation have provided safe harbor as I interviewed and as we broke bread. Each poem is dedicated to the memory of Black descendants that worked and lived on the lands of rural America and the rural south. Some of the poems were first performed at the Wallace House for Arts and Reconciliation special programs for the public.

I am ever grateful to Nell Gottlieb, Peter Datcher, Theo Perkins, and all administrators of the Wallace House and the History House in Shelby County, Alabama. Your warm invitation into the history and love of your people brought this book into the light.

I am in gratitude to my family in Greensboro, Alabama for always encouraging me to speak and tell stories. Your love and support have helped me to continue toward the vision of writing about rural America. I also thank my early writing groups as I sat on Lucy's red couch and found poetry and listened to the most talented writers and friends. I have special appreciation to Lucy, Margaret, Lori, Melanie, Kathy, and my dearly departed Alison, and many others throughout the years who supported me in my writing career.

I thank Pulley Press for taking a chance on a new author and forging the vision of this work into the world. I am ever indebted to my editor Frances. Frances, thank you for your time, tenderness, and glorious gestures of encouragement. With your guidance and care I am better, this book is better, our words are better together.

Lastly, I want to thank the evolving imaginations and memories of Black women who helped me to acknowledge the woman in the yellow apron and to all of those enslaved who welcomed me into their revivals. Love became air through the breath of each poem and poetic voice that entered the walls and dared to offer freedom. I walk in gratitude to the spirit of revival and this book is dedicated to that spirit and the holy awe of joy reclaimed.

Notes

Many of the poems were created during Homecoming days at
the Wallace House. Wallace Center for Arts and Reconciliation
Homecoming occurs yearly on the second Saturday of October.
Black and white descendants reunite for ceremony, remembrance,
and a dedication to descendants on the property and at the
cemetery where Black and white descendants are buried in
separate locations.

The Laying of the Wreath—*Laying of the Wreath in memory of loved ones.
During Homecoming 2024 a wreath was placed at the cemetery of Black
descendants from the Wallace House Plantation for Troy Datcher upon his
passing, Troy was at the prior Homecoming in 2023. Henry Smith, elder Black
descendant stated these words while laying the wreath upon dedication to
those loved ones who passed:*

"We lay this wreath for all slaves that are buried here in Wallace
Cemetery. They are known to us because when they died, no one
thought enough to put a marker or anything on the grave, although
they are known to us, they are known to our Lord and Savior."

June 2023 (Juneteenth) the first Black Descendants Day was
proclaimed on the grounds of the Wallace House. Juneteenth
commemorates June 18, 1865 when a union general arrived to
enforce the Emancipation Proclamation in Texas, months after

the Civil War. The holiday commemorates the end of slavery in the United States. Over 70 Black descendants celebrated at the house for the first time solely as Black descendants.

Author Biography

SALAAM GREEN is the inaugural poet laureate of historic Birmingham, Alabama, 2024–2025. The prestigious position recognizes Ms. Green's outstanding contributions to the literary arts and her commitment to fostering a deeper appreciation for poetry within our community. She was born in the Black Belt of Alabama and was raised by a family of educators and a single mother. Despite growing up in rural Alabama with limited resources, she was encouraged by her mother, a retired teacher, to read, write, and dream for a better future. She graduated from the University of Montevallo with an English degree and has a MS in Early Childhood Education from the University of North Dakota graduate program and has spent more than 16 years as an arts educator, healer, and community leader.

Green, Literary Arts Awardee 2024, is the founder and director of Literary Healing Arts and a Road Scholar for the Alabama Humanities Alliance. A certified trainer for the Kellogg Foundation's Truth, Racial Healing & Transformation initiative, she also leads "Write to Heal" workshops—a series of seminars geared at instructing both individuals and organizations in using poetry, writing, and storytelling to reclaim their voices and transform their lives. In 2018, Green helped conduct a series of "Truth Booths" during the massive For Freedoms public art project, where she guided participants through conversations about social and environmental justice. Green has garnered esteemed residencies including University of Alabama at Birmingham Arts in Medicine, The Wallace House for Arts and Reconciliation, and the Auburn University Jule Collins Smith Museum. Green is a published author, sought-out speaker, and TEDx Birmingham alumnus speaker whose work has been featured in the *Alabama Arts Journal*, *Southern Women's Review*, *Scalawag* and more.